ALL ABOUT SATELLITES

Miriam Gross

PowerKiDS
press.

New York

Published in 2009 by The Rosen Publishing Group, Inc.
29 East 21st Street, New York, NY 10010

Copyright © 2009 by The Rosen Publishing Group, Inc.

First Edition

Editor: Joanne Randolph
Book Design: Greg Tucker
Photo Research: Jessica Gerweck

Photo Credits: Cover © Michael Dunning/Getty Images; pp. 5, 7, 13, 19, 21 © Getty Images; p. 9 © AFP/Getty Images; pp. 11, 15 © Associated Press; p. 17 Shutterstock.com.

Library of Congress Cataloging-in-Publication Data

Gross, Miriam J.
  All about satellites / Miriam Gross. — 1st ed.
     p. cm. — (Blast off!)
  Includes bibliographical references and index.
  ISBN 978-1-4358-2736-3 (library binding) — ISBN 978-1-4358-3134-6 (pbk.)
ISBN 978-1-4358-3140-7 (6-pack)
  1. Artificial satellites—Juvenile literature. I. Title.
  TL796.3.G76 2009
  629.46—dc22
                                        2008029036

Manufactured in the United States of America

CONTENTS

WHAT IS A SATELLITE?   4

AROUND AND AROUND   6

SPUTNIK   8

THE FIRST AMERICAN SATELLITES   10

SENDING MESSAGES THROUGH SPACE   12

STORM WATCHERS   14

SEEING EARTH FROM SPACE   16

WHAT ELSE IS OUT THERE?   18

A HOME IN SPACE   20

SPACE POWER   22

GLOSSARY   23

INDEX   24

WEB SITES   24

What's that light shining in the night sky? It looks like a star, but it moves across the sky. That traveling light is likely from a satellite.

A satellite is an object that moves in a circle around a larger object. Some satellites are natural. The Moon is a natural satellite to Earth. Other satellites are man-made, or artificial. People **launch** these satellites into space with rockets. Sometimes they are used to study outer space. Other satellites help us use telephones or watch TV. Some satellites are used as a home for astronauts in space. Around 3,000 working satellites fly around Earth.

This is one of the United States' tracking and data relay satellites. These satellites track satellites in orbit. They also send and receive data, or facts, from Earth.

The path that a satellite takes around an object is called its orbit. In order to stay in orbit, a satellite must move at just the right speed. If it moves too slowly, it would be pulled down to Earth by **gravity**. If it moves too quickly, it would fly out into space.

Sometimes old satellites start to slow down in orbit. This makes them fall to Earth. As they fall, satellites often break apart or burn up. Sometimes the broken pieces continue orbiting as "space junk." Pieces of space junk are satellites, too.

This man holds a tile from a space shuttle, which is a spacecraft that flies into space more then once. Objects like this tile that float in space are called space junk.

The first artificial satellite was called *Sputnik*. It was launched by the **Soviet Union** on October 4, 1957. *Sputnik* means "fellow traveler" in Russian. It looked like a silver ball with four **antennae** coming out of it.

Sputnik traveled at nearly 5 miles per second (8 km/s). It made a full circle around Earth every 96 minutes. Inside, *Sputnik* carried gear to send a **signal** back to Earth. All over the world, people could hear *Sputnik*'s "beep-beep" signal on their radios. *Sputnik* orbited Earth for three months and then broke apart.

Here you can see the ball-shaped *Sputnik* and its four antennae. The silver covering on the satellite was made to withstand huge amounts of heat.

The United States launched its first satellite on January 31, 1958. *Explorer 1* was shaped like a pencil. It weighed 31.7 pounds (14.4 kg) and was 80.7 inches (2 m) long.

Explorer 1 carried gear to study space. It recorded tiny space objects called micrometeoroids. It also measured **radiation** in space. *Explorer 1* stayed in orbit until 1970.

On March 17, 1958, the United States launched *Vanguard 1*. It measured only 6.4 inches (16.3 cm) across and weighed 3.2 pounds (1.5 kg). *Vanguard 1* was powered by solar cells, which turn **energy** from the Sun into electricity. It still orbits Earth today.

This is a close-up picture of *Vanguard 1* taken about a month before its launch. The

Communications satellites relay signals. This means they receive signals from one point on Earth and send them out to other places.

The first communications satellite was called *Echo*. It was launched in August 1960. *Echo* was 98 feet (30 m) wide. It looked like a giant silver balloon. *Echo* sent TV signals from New Jersey to California.

Today, there are hundreds of communications satellites in orbit. They help us communicate by telephone, Internet, and TV. They let people stay in touch with people in almost every country on Earth.

This is the *Syncom IV-5* communications satellite. It is a special kind of satellite that seems to stay in the same spot above Earth at all times.

Some satellites are used to take pictures of Earth from high above the clouds. These pictures can be used to study Earth's weather. They can tell us when storms are coming. Weather satellites can also measure how warm or cool the air is.

The first weather satellites were part of the Tiros system. The United States launched 10 Tiros satellites between 1960 and 1965. Each of these satellites had two special cameras that took 32 pictures of Earth during every orbit. Today, satellites in the World Weather Watch system provide continuous reports on weather over the whole world.

This is a photo of *Tiros 1* after its launch in 1960. This satellite had cameras and other tools to track weather on Earth.

Satellite pictures help us keep people safe from major storms, such as hurricanes. Satellites can also help us make better maps of our cities and plan where to build our roads and railways.

Satellites can also show us how Earth is changing. We can see how our cities are growing and where forests have been cut down. We can see what kinds of crops grow on farms and how much food the world is growing. Satellites can also show us air **pollution** over cities and oil pollution in the sea. Seeing Earth from high above can help us plan how to better take care of it.

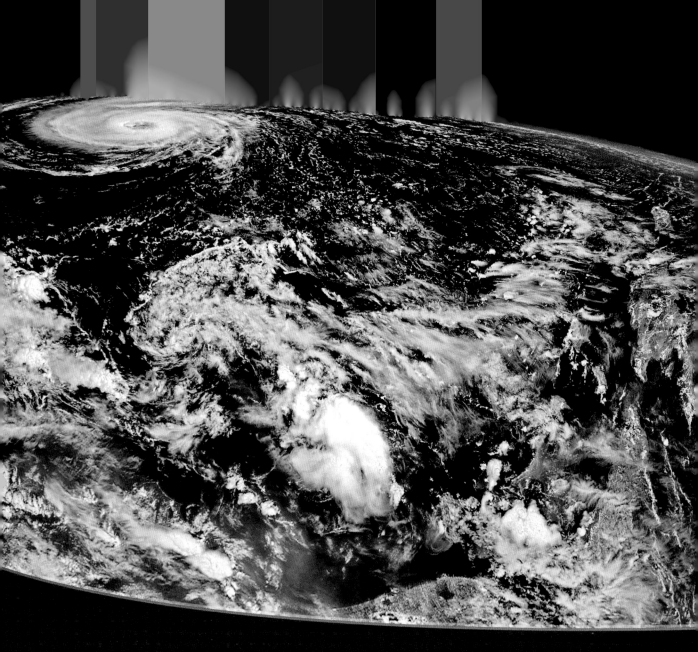

Satellites can take pictures of Earth that help us track big storms. This is a satellite

Scientific satellites can help us learn more about what the **universe** is made of, and where it came from. Some of these satellites orbit Earth. Some of them orbit other **planets**, or even the Sun.

Some satellites measure what happens to the Sun's energy as it travels through space. Others study matter in space near Earth.

When satellites orbit other planets, they can take pictures and send them to Earth. This allows us to see much more than we can from Earth. Satellites have shown us that there is ice on Mars. They have also made maps of Venus.

The Hubble Space Telescope took this photo of Mars. The Hubble Space Telescope is a satellite that was put into orbit in 1990.

Space stations are satellites that orbit Earth while people live and work inside. Most space stations orbit at 200 to 300 miles (322–483 km) above Earth. **Astronauts** fly up to the space station in a spacecraft called the space shuttle.

The International Space Station is the largest man-made satellite in history. It weighs 404,000 pounds (183,251 kg) and is as long as a football field. This satellite takes 91 minutes to orbit Earth. It shines brighter than the stars. Maybe you will be lucky enough to catch sight of it one night!

This is the ISS as it looked in 2006. It was launched in 1998, and it will take many

Satellites may one day help provide electricity for Earth to use. These solar power satellites would catch energy from the Sun. They would then send it down to Earth where it can be turned into electricity. Since the Sun does not set in space, solar energy can be gathered 24 hours a day, and there are no clouds to block it.

Satellites might also be used as power stations in space. They could use the Sun's energy to power spacecraft and other satellites that have run low on electricity. This way, spacecraft can travel farther into outer space.

GLOSSARY

ANTENNAE (an-TEH-nee) Metal objects used to send and receive signals.

ASTRONAUTS (AS-troh-nots) People who are trained to travel in outer space.

COMMUNICATIONS (kuh-myoo-nih-KAY-shunz) The sharing of facts, feelings, or messages.

ENERGY (EH-nur-jee) The power to work or act.

GRAVITY (GRA-vih-tee) The natural force that causes objects to move toward the center of Earth.

LAUNCH (LONCH) To push out or to put into the air.

PLANETS (PLA-nets) Large objects, such as Earth, that move around the Sun.

POLLUTION (puh-LOO-shun) Bad matter.

RADIATION (ray-dee-AY-shun) Rays of light, heat, or energy that spread outward from something.

SIGNAL (SIG-nul) A message, movement, or sound that is sent to be read by others.

SOVIET UNION (SOH-vee-et YOON-yun) A former country that reached from eastern Europe across Asia to the Pacific Ocean.

UNIVERSE (YOO-nih-vers) All of space.

C
cities, 16
communications satellite,
    12

E
Echo, 12
Explorer 1, 10

I
International Space Station
    (ISS), 20

M
maps, 16
Mars, 18

O
orbit, 6, 10, 12, 14, 18, 20

P
pollution, 16

R
radiation, 10
rockets, 4

S
solar cells, 10
Soviet Union, 8
space junk, 6
space stations, 20
Sputnik, 8

T
Tiros system, 14

V
Vanguard 1, 10
Venus, 18

W
weather satellites, 14

WEB SITES

Due to the changing nature of Internet links, PowerKids Press has developed an online list of Web sites related to the subject of this book. This site is updated regularly. Please use this link to access the list:
www.powerkidslinks.com/blastoff/satellites/